Ethereum

A Complete Blueprint to Understanding and Profiting with Ethereum

☐ **Copyright 2017 by Brian T Smith - All rights reserved.**

This document is geared towards providing exact and reliable information in regards to the topic and issue covered. The publication is sold with the idea that the publisher is not required to render accounting, officially permitted, or otherwise, qualified services. If advice is necessary, legal or professional, a practiced individual in the profession should be ordered.

- From a Declaration of Principles which was accepted and approved equally by a Committee of the American Bar Association and a Committee of Publishers and Associations.

In no way is it legal to reproduce, duplicate, or transmit any part of this document in either electronic means or in printed format. Recording of this publication is strictly prohibited and any storage of this document is not allowed unless with written permission from the publisher. All rights reserved.

The information provided herein is stated to be truthful and consistent, in that any liability, in terms of inattention or otherwise, by any usage or abuse of any policies, processes, or directions contained within is the solitary and utter responsibility of the recipient reader. Under no circumstances will any legal responsibility or blame be held against the publisher for any reparation, damages, or monetary loss due to the information herein, either directly or indirectly.

Respective authors own all copyrights not held by the publisher.

The information herein is offered for informational purposes solely, and is universal as so. The presentation of the information is without contract or any type of guarantee assurance.

The trademarks that are used are without any consent, and the publication of the trademark is without permission or backing by the trademark owner. All trademarks and brands within this book are for clarifying purposes only and are the owned by the owners themselves, not affiliated with this document.

Table of Contents

Introduction 5

Chapter One: What Are Cryptocurrency, Bitcoin, Ethereum and Money? 7

Chapter Two: What is Blockchain? 16

Chapter Three: What is Ethereum? 21

Chapter Four: The Technology Engine behind Ethereum 25

Chapter Five: What is the future of Ethereum? 34

Chapter Six: Ethereum KeyPlayers and Technical Infrastructure 45

Chapter Seven: How Do I Go About Investing In Ethereum? 47

Conclusion 63

Other Books 64

Introduction

A few sentences concerning the book, *"Ethereum"* This book contains essential information, as you investigate Ethereum. As you start this book, try to answer these questions:

- What do you know about cryptocurrency? What do you know about money?
- What do you know about Ethereum and its underlying technology called blockchain?
- Do you know there is far more to Ethereum than there is to Bitcoin? Some see it as being as revolutionary in our time as the Internet was in the last decade of the last century.
- Do you realize how Ethereum is transforming many inefficient and bureaucratic procedures? Are you aware of its potential for changing nearly everything?
- Do you know the tremendous investment opportunities arising from Ethereum?
- Do you need to be informed about sensible investment procedures, particularly with any type of cryptocurrency?

This small book tells you about them in as simple a manner as it can. It does so in a way that is inspiring and will make you realize that Ethereum and its blockchain empowers people to improve their financial futures. This book is meant for the layperson; it has not been written for those who are already expert in blockchain technology and cryptocurrency. Even they, though, may find much of interest in the book, which is a mine of information and full of ideas.

It has seven chapters:
Each chapter is self-contained but leads on to the next in a logical way.

Ready to get involved? Onto Chapter 1.

Chapter One: What Are Cryptocurrency, Bitcoin, Ethereum and Money?

Cryptocurrency! What is it? Using the encryption techniques of cryptography and cutting edge computing it is possible to create money that is called *cryptocurrency*. Money is a store of value; it must be transferable and transfers must be capable of verification.

Cryptocurrency has these features. It also has something else, which has significantly enhanced its appeal, for many, and that is its complete independence from any government or central bank. Cryptocurrencies are decentralized, with no central authority controlling them.

Recently, most large banks have become involved with the technology that has allowed cryptocurrencies to flourish. However such currency as comes from them will be controlled by these banks and will not be cryptocurrency. The original creators of cryptocurrency were insistent there must never be such centralization.

The development of cryptocurrencies: Bitcoin was the first cryptocurrency and has been the subject of much publicity; its value in dollar terms has considerably increased in the last couple of years. As well as Bitcoin, there are a lot of other cryptocurrencies, one of which, Ethereum, is the subject of this book.

Many of these cryptocurrencies have also had a great increase in their dollar value. Government and legitimate business have an ever-increasing involvement in cryptocurrency and there is a huge market for these currencies, with the market capitalization of all cryptocurrencies in late August 2017 more than $150,000,000,000!

Facts about cryptocurrency: During the latter part of 2017, there were more than 1100 cryptocurrencies. Bitcoin, the cryptocurrency with greatest market capitalization, has received much unfortunate attention because recent hacking attacks on organizations around the world have demanded Bitcoins as ransom. Many in the criminal world believe payments in cryptocurrency are untraceable. In fact, this is only partially true.

If you want to see all sorts of intriguing things about cryptocurrency, then log onto the website *coinmarketcap*. Each of the top 100 cryptocurrencies, by market capitalization, has a little graph next to it, revealing the fluctuation of its value, in US$, during the last seven days. You can also find the change in the value as a percentage in the last 24 hours. If your interest concerns all cryptocurrencies, then there is another table showing a great many more cryptocurrencies, with the same information, but minus the graphs.

Another site, with valuable information about cryptocurrencies, is *worldcoinindex*. This site is similar to *coinmarketcap*. However, it is not identical and does not have the same information but should be a reference for anyone interested in cryptocurrency.

Checking one of these shows that Bitcoin (BTC) has a large proportion, nearly 50% of the total capitalization. Its actual market capitalization was more than $70 billion (US). One BTC had a value during August 2017 of $4300. Other cryptocurrencies also had large market capitalizations and values.

Ethereum (ETH), the subject of this book, had market capitalization greater than $30 billion and one Ether (ETH), the coin of Ethereum, had a value more than $330. Not all cryptocurrencies by a large market capitalization have coins of high value; an example is Ripple (XRP) whose rank in market capitalization is about fourth with a value of $8 billion. However, 1 XRP only had a value of about $0.2 (US) at that time.

The reader may think that all cryptocurrencies have high market capitalization. This belief is not true, as a check of all cryptocurrencies shows. At the same time that Bitcoin, Ethereum, and Ripple had the values listed, another cryptocurrency Digital Coin (DMB) had a market capitalization $455 (US), and there were many others much lower than this. We will discuss this myriad of coins and how they arise later.

How is cryptocurrency created? In the first paragraph, we said this creation used the encryption techniques of cryptography and cutting edge computing technology. Expanding on this, we can compare a cryptocurrency to an incorruptible digital ledger. All financial dealings in this currency are recorded in the ledger. A large number of powerful computers called *nodes* maintain this ledger. The network of nodes maintains the *blockchain* and the next chapter has much greater detail about it. We call the process of producing cryptocurrencies *mining*.

Mining of cryptocurrencies: It is an intriguing fact that there will never be more than 21,000,000 Bitcoins. When Bitcoins are made the process by which this occurs is called *mining*. The initial Bitcoiners, Satoshi Nakamoto and Hal Finney, were able to mine Bitcoins using desktop computers, but as more and more Bitcoins were produced mining required computers of much greater power.

This problem is caused by the use of *hash functions*, which are mathematical objects that are very difficult for lay people to wrap their heads around and discussed far more thoroughly later. Most cryptocurrencies arise from similar mining and this includes Ether, the coin of Ethereum, subject of this book.

Unlike Bitcoin, the number of Ethereum is unlimited, although the total number of Ether possible each year is about 18 million. However, Ethereum does not have a *hard cap*, which is a maximum number of coins. This lack of a hard cap may cause problems in the future.

Cryptocurrency, stocks and ordinary money: With the word cryptocurrency used to signify electronic money, the reader may wonder what the term is for the currencies in our daily lives such as the dollar, euro (Europe) or renminbi (China). The term used by those involved with cryptocurrency is *fiat currency*.

In some ways, cryptocurrency resembles the stocks and shares of the stock market than money, as most of us are accustomed to using. Currently, most cryptocurrencies need purchase from cryptocurrency exchanges in the same way that someone buys stocks and shares from a stock exchange. The acquisition of a cryptocurrency is the buying of part of the digital computer network for that currency and an entry in the blockchain of that cryptocurrency.

Is cryptocurrency different to money?
Earlier we said that money is a store of value that it must be transferable and the transfers must be

capable of verification. Cryptocurrency has these latter two features. However, if you have looked at coinmarketcap, you would see great fluctuations in the value of all cryptocurrencies. It is probably fair to say that cryptocurrency is not yet a reliable store of value.

In countries, which are politically or socially unstable, the currencies are not reliable stores of value. Most cryptocurrencies resemble the currency of unstable countries with the worth not consistent. In 2017, most cryptocurrency is bought for speculative reasons and with the high increases in the values of the major cryptocurrencies, this is not a serious problem. However, a significant downturn in the values of these currencies could cause a crisis, if too many people invest too great a proportion of their wealth in cryptocurrency.

Does cryptocurrency have advantages over fiat money? These have been present from Bitcoin's inception.
- Cryptocurrencies, usually have the benefit of complete decentralization. No nation, business or bank control them.
- Cryptocurrencies rely on their blockchain and its nodes. Failure of some nodes will not prevent the

continuation of the currency. This reliability is similar to the Internet.
- When most cryptocurrencies are used in transactions, there is greater anonymity and privacy than using fiat currencies. However, having said that, there is now a belief that cryptocurrencies are about as anonymous and private as cash. Governments are using some of the best computing experts to find ways of unraveling transactions in cryptocurrency.
- Initially, cryptocurrencies may seem strange. However, usually, with practice in using them, they become as simple as fiat money.
- Cryptocurrencies are, for many, much cheaper and quicker than fiat currencies with their fees and delays in the completion of transactions.
- With cryptocurrency, there is no danger of *charge back*, where a dissatisfied customer is allowed cancel a transaction that involves credit cards. This lack of chargeback is a feature of great appeal to traders.
- A useful feature of cryptocurrencies is that as a result of their electronic nature they are far more robust and portable than cash and notes.
- Fraud is much less probable with cryptocurrency than with fiat money, which, sadly, now suffers from frequent theft by hackers of credit card numbers and subsequent sale on the Internet.

Blockchain: We discussed this previously and just mention that when we write blockchain, we are using a shortened version of writing blockchain technology. By use of this, the distribution of digital information, without the threat of being copied, is possible. When it first began blockchain was only for the use of Bitcoin, which was the first and is still the largest cryptocurrency.

Blockchain, as with all new technologies, has new uses being discovered for it every day. Initially blockchain, through Bitcoin, was visualized as a way to overcome the deficiencies of the global banking system that nearly caused a financial meltdown in 2007-2008.

Nowadays, we know that this technology has applications far beyond money and finance. Ethereum fulfills this realization, and future chapters of this book will illustrate how this amazing technology is doing this.

Chapter Two: What is Blockchain?

The blockchain is similar to a massive Excel-like spreadsheet, distributed over a network of computers called nodes, each node with a copy of the spreadsheet. During each hour, there are frequent updates of this ledger; as a consequence, the ledger always possesses correct information. In many ways the blockchain is a whole lot of massive, distributed, interacting databases called nodes. It is the distributed nature of the blockchain that makes it so valuable. Interactions occur using what are called *protocols*. These are rules written into the software.

One of the benefits is that there is never centralization of records; the records are public and on any node. It is impossible for hackers to direct focus attacks at one point, which is their usual modus operandi. A hacker would have to access to the complete network to fulfill their nefarious schemes, and that is not possible.

Proceeding with the giant spreadsheet analogy is very useful in understanding this technology. Normally, when we use a spreadsheet it is unavailable for others; they are locked out. With *Google Sheets* of *Google Docs* this locking out does not occur, allowing others to work on the same sheet, at the same time that we are working on it. The blockchain is similar except that the spreadsheet is not centralized and under the control of one organization such as Google, or Alphabet as they are now called.

What is blockchain? The blockchain is a real time computing application distributed over a network, often described as peer-to-peer. Blockchain uses cryptography and digital signatures to prove identity and enforce read/write privileges. With its data spread over many nodes, the validity of the data is far more secure from hackers than with centralized storage.

We can compare the blockchain to the Internet. It possesses both flexibility and toughness. It has identical blocks of information stored throughout the nodes on the network; there is no point in the network where failure would bring the network to its knees.

No further proof of this required than the success of Bitcoin. It has been in more or less continual operation since 2009 and has had no significant disruption. Such troubles as having occurred, are the result of human stupidity, incompetence and error. Blockchain technology has been thoroughly tested and proved. It is not an experimental technology although some of the applications built with it are.

Let us continue this comparison between the Internet and the blockchain. The Internet came to life, near the end of the 1960s at the height of the Cold War, so that it could survive a nuclear attack. It was only for military purposes. However, its use spread to universities and government. Finally, during the 1990s, it became commercially available. In spite of almost 30 years of uninterrupted use, the Internet has worked marvelously. The blockchain is in the same situation now that the Internet was in the 1990s. Many predict that its effects will be even more revolutionary than that of the Internet.

What the nodes of a blockchain are: As it is so important, we repeat that the nodes of a blockchain are the computers with the databases containing the ledger. The nodes transmit through the network details of any changes occurring in them. The changes are recorded in the blockchain. All nodes verify any transaction. The verification by one node is entirely independent of the audit by any other node. It is important to remember that the whole blockchain is updated every few minutes. No large centralized computer controls it; the updating process automatically occurs throughout the blockchain network.

The blocks of blockchain? The writing of new transactions to the blockchain takes during *mining*. We use the word blockchain, as there is a chain of *blocks* containing the transactions. Mining, and thus the manufacture of the blocks, needs very powerful computers. The miners make new coins in conjunction with making the blocks.

As mining takes place, an agreement is reached automatically between nodes. A transaction is written into the blockchain when a majority of nodes agree on the transaction's validity. Earlier it was mentioned that the process of mining requires the solution of very complex problems in mathematics. The nodes that do this are called the *miners*. We repeat that transactions are recorded in parts of the ledger called *blocks*.

A block is a table that has a timestamp; a reference, named the *height*, to the previously mined block, the transactions recorded in the block and the problem that miners had to solve. Anyone can see the Ethereum blockchain, as it is modified, by visiting the site etherscan.io/blocks. With this site, it is possible to see the information contained in the Ethereum blockchain. A click on any number from the Height column reveals a lot of information about that block's contents.

Doing this shows the word *hash* as the name of the fourth row. This word is of great importance as it is the result of a *hash function*. A hash function transforms a transaction to a 256-bit number, which is called a *hash number* and is then placed in a block after the nodes validate the hash.

The mining process assigns a unique hash number to each transaction. The chance of any two transactions with the same hash number is infinitesimally small as the number of possible hashes is so vast. Such a process is called *collision resistant*.

Chapter Three: What is Ethereum?

More than anything else Ethereum is a platform for developing blockchain applications. This fact about Ethereum accounts for its importance and is central to the incredible success of Ethereum.

Ethereum's early history: Vitalik Buterin proposed Ethereum in a whitepaper written in 2013. Buterin is an extraordinarily gifted young Russian, born in 1994, who is only 23 years old. In 2000, his parents emigrated from Russia to Canada for better opportunities and where Vitalik received most of his education.

While at school, it soon became apparent that he had a flair for mathematics and computing. His father, who was a computer scientist, taught Vitalik about Bitcoin. Vitalik was fascinated and saw possibilities for blockchain, far beyond its commercial use in Bitcoin, the extraordinarily successful cryptocurrency.

He wrote his paper and ended up leaving his university studies at the University of Waterloo in Ontario to work full-time on Ethereum. A core team of four members, including Buterin, started the development of the Ethereum software project. Development money was provided by crowdfunding, using payments in Bitcoins.

The Ethereum concept was always lauded for its brilliance, but from the very outset, there were serious questions about its scalability and its security. Ethereum was launched in July 2015 and has proceeded through four versions since then, with Olympic version 0, Frontier version 1, Homestead version 2 and the next version 3, which is Metropolis due late September 2017. There are plans for a version 4, called Serenity.

Concerns about security proved well-founded, as in 2016, an organization called DAO, which stands for decentralized autonomous organization, a set of smart contracts (we will discuss these later) based on the Ethereum platform raised $150 million to crowdfund itself. Sadly, a hacker was able to raid the DAO and steal $50 million (US). This disaster caused a split in the Ethereum community and led to the creation of two types of Ethereum. Ethereum (ETH), which is the subject of this book, and

Ethereum Classic (ETC), a cryptocurrency with a market capitalization of nearly $1.5 billion (US).

The split was the result of what is called a *hard fork* in blockchain technology. A hard fork is where in block chain technology the protocols for mining and transactions are altered so that previously invalid blocks and transactions become valid or vice versa. The effect of a hard fork is that all nodes must now use upgrades to software to use the new protocols.

A hard fork is similar to a schism in religion but on a technical level. At this point, it is worth mentioning what a *soft fork* is. A soft fork occurs where previously valid blocks or transactions become invalid. The difference between hard forks and soft forks is very technical, and we will not dwell on this difference.

In this book, we have described the mechanics of blockchain, which makes Ethereum possible. However, the reader may be wondering why Ethereum? Why not just use Bitcoin? Bitcoin has been around for eight years and is gaining ever more support, why not just use it?

The answer is quite simple. Bitcoin is first and foremost money and fulfills this purpose brilliantly. With Ethereum it is important never to forget the words from the beginning of this chapter,' *More than anything else, Ethereum is a platform for developing blockchain applications.*' Such blockchain applications are called *smart contracts*.

Smart contracts are in essence digital exchange processes. The blockchain, which gave rise to transactions using cryptocurrency, is capable of all sorts of value exchanges. With this technology, the checking, execution and security of a vast number of these are possible.

The means of doing this is by the use of dApps (distributed applications), written in computing languages, such well-known languages as C, JavaScript of websites and Python and languages specially designed for Ethereum, such as the Solidity language. In computing jargon, the dApps used in developing smart contracts produce what are called high-level programming objects. The Ethereum blockchain processes these. The technology for this will be explored far more thoroughly in a future chapter, in this chapter it is sufficient to be aware of the existence of smart contracts.

Chapter Four: The Technology Engine behind Ethereum

Ethereum facilitates peer-to-peer electronic transactions, without an intermediary. Ethereum's smart contracts ensure that if somebody wants to execute a process and do something, then that person should only do what they are entitled to do. All actions are recorded in the blockchain, and any attempts to do more than is permitted is checked then stopped by the network of nodes.

Every node joins all other nodes of the blockchain. On receipt of information about a new action, these checks, to verify the proposed action, are made automatically:

- What is the action that the sender of the information proposes?
- Is the sender authorized to carry out this action?
- If the action is legitimate, can it be done?

The node that contains the information can carry out this check using its copy of the blockchain. The node sends its decision concerning the legitimacy of the action to all the other nodes. If most nodes agree about the action's validity action, it gets recorded.

Ethereum does this using blockchain technology, among the most important features of this are the following parts.

Encryption: Here is how encryption works. If X makes contact with Y to do something, Y transmits to X, often oblivious to this communication, a *public key*. X often is ignorant this public key has come but proceeds and carries out the action desired by Y.

The public key works on the file, which contains the result of the action, and transforms it into a form that is indecipherable. Once completed, X transmits the file, which has been encrypted to Y. During the transmission all that someone who intercepted it would see is an unreadable mess, as a result of encryption.

When Y gets this, it is encrypted. However, Y possesses, often unknowingly, something called a private key, which acts on the encrypted file so that Y can read *Y*it.

For most people, it is unnecessary to comprehend how encryption works. However, if you want some idea about how it does then it is necessary to cast your mind back to high school and mathematics. There you probably learned about prime numbers.

These are numbers that have only two numbers that divide into the number without a remainder, 1 and the number itself. Simple examples are 2,3 and 11; 1 and 2 can only divide the number 2, if there is to be no remainder; 1 and 3 can only divide the number 3 if there is to be no remainder; 1 and 11 can only divide the number 11 if there is to be no remainder.

Another very important property of prime numbers is that the set of them is infinite so that no matter how big a prime number you have there will always be a bigger one. This is very important for encryption.

Most whole numbers are products of prime numbers. If such a number is quite small then a computer can find the primes that multiplied to give the number quite quickly but if the number is the product of two very large primes then even the most powerful computer in the world would take centuries to find the primes which were multiplied to get that number. It is this property of prime numbers on which all encryption is currently based.

The public and private keys are generated by prime numbers and they are able to act on each other to give the underlying message. It is a frightening thought that if computers got a lot more powerful than they are now then this method of encryption would not work and a new method would have to be devised.

Hash Functions: Hash functions take various data and always convert it to data of a fixed size. Here is a piece of data on a block on the Ethereum blockchain
0x1dcc4de8dec75d7aab85b567b6ccd41ad312451b948a7413f0a142fd40d49347

Here is another

0x29583ca1fc5a14675f9e72ff4948c6600ddc093e

Not every piece of data gets changed to a similar length piece of data on the same block as there are different hash functions at work on a block depending on their role.

When transactions are put onto a block they get put onto the same block throughout the blockchain on every node. There has to be agreement among the nodes. This is how security works on the blockchain.

To show how this works, we have an elementary basic hash function on strings of letters. This hash function takes or in mathematical terms maps *a* -> 2, *b* -> 3, ...,*z* -> 27 then only takes the first five alternate letters, beginning with the second then the fourth, etc.

The sentence," *I will do as you say*," would be transformed in the following way.

I will do as you say -> *I will do as yo* (as we only deal with the first *five* alternate letters, we only need the first 11 letters)

I will do as yo -> 10 24 10 11 11 5 2 20 26 16 (exchanging numbers for letters)

10 24 10 11 11 5 2 20 26 16 ->24 11 5 20 16 (only picking alternate numbers starting from second)

With collapsing of the spaces, we get the hash number 241152016.

The hash function in this one case worked as follows if we call our hash function *hash* (".....").

Hash ("*I will do as you say* ") = 241152016.

How do hash functions fit into Ethereum? The Ethereum blockchain consists of blocks, which are the creation of miners solving mathematics problems of high complexity. As they create the blocks, they use transactions that are unconfirmed. The transactions that they use go in these blocks. These transactions go into their block in a hashed form. The transactions of one person will usually be in different blocks; this is always the case if their transactions occur at different times.

This short description of the mathematics of the Ethereum blockchain is not quite finished as we have to discuss *nonce number*.

Nonce number: If we use Ethereum then each transaction has a nonce number. The nonce records the number of transactions sent from any particular address. Each time you send a transaction from this address the nonce increases by one. This is quite straightforward but it has implications for miners using transactions. The blocks receive transactions in order of nonce. Transactions with a nonce of 0 get placed ahead of those with nonce of 1, which in turn go ahead of those with nonce of 2 etc. The reason for this order is the prevention of double spending.

A nonce is a number that occurs once in every hash. This affords more protection, as each time we use hash functions, they will give different results. One of the reasons for this to prevent a hacking attack named a *replay attack*.

Have we covered everything?

If you consult Wikipedia or some other reference, you will be informed,
'*Ethereum is a blockchain-using platform, which is public, open-source, and allows the scripting of smart contracts. The EVM (Ethereum Virtual Machine) executes these scripts are on its network of nodes. The EVM is a Turing-complete virtual machine that is decentralized.*' or words to this effect.

In this chapter, we have talked about the mathematics involved in encryption and the hashing of information, which gets placed in the blocks.
However, there are two terms in the description that need to be defined, as they have not been talked about before.

Turing-complete: The term Turing-complete can be hard to understand but is quite straightforward. In layperson's terms, a computer program or computer platform is Turing-complete if it can do anything that is programmable. A simple calculator is not Turing-complete as it can only execute programs associated with arithmetic.

As far as we know, it is not possible to write a computer program to simulate falling in love, so it would not be possible do that on a Turing-complete platform. However, if you can write a program on a machine to do any action, which is programmable then that machine is Turing-complete. Ethereum is Turing-complete but Bitcoin is not. The Bitcoin program is designed only for financial calculations and transactions. This gives Ethereum its great value but it makes it more vulnerable.

Ethereum Virtual Machine: The Ethereum Virtual Machine is a computer programming environment, which runs on every node of the Ethereum blockchain. It is capable of carrying out any smart contract, written on it. The Ethereum Virtual Machine is Turing-complete.

Summary: The development of Ethereum has been progressing steadily since 2015. It carries out transactions and uses a blockchain that consists of a network of blocks, which are created by the miners and are maintained by the nodes. Transactions are encrypted. The blocks contain the hashes of all confirmed transactions. Miners utilize unconfirmed transactions to create new blocks. Each time a transaction takes place that transaction will use a nonce number to keep the transaction secure. A hash of a transaction goes in the blockchain after it is confirmed. This happens after most nodes are in agreement about its validity and reach consensus.

Chapter Five: What is the future of Ethereum?

Ethereum should have a very bright future. Remember the words at the beginning of Chapter 3, 'More than anything else is Ethereum is a platform for developing blockchain applications.' It is Turing-complete. If something can be programmed, then it can be programmed on the Ethereum platform.

The following are a few of the many applications using Ethereum or similar.

Identity Verification: Identity verification occupies too much time and effort currently. By means, which use the decentralization of blockchains, such as Ethereum, it will be much quicker to verify online identity. The risks to online identity data, held in a central location, will vanish with the use of the Ethereum smart contracts. Centralized points of vulnerability for computer hackers to attack will disappear.

This protection results from the public and private keys system of the encryption in Ethereum. The user's address is the public key, a huge string of numbers and letters. Transmission through the network uses that address. The password giving the owner ability to use their cryptocurrency or other digital assets is the *private key*.

Data stored using Ethereum is tamper proof and incorruptible. Vulnerabilities will occur if the owner stores their private key in such a way that hackers and others can get hold of it.

Throughout the world, the power of the Ethereum blockchain in improving the process of identity verification is being trialed and realized. Here are some examples.

The city of Zug in Switzerland has specifically gone for a decentralized application (DAPP) to verify the electronic identity of its citizens, in preference to some centralized method. The president of Zug has stated the city's need for a single electronic identity for each of its citizens, for all possible purposes and he has declared the city's wish that the digital identity must not be centralized in the city. The development of this DAPP uses the Uport identity platform of the ConsensSys Ethereum organization as well as input from others in academe and business.

Another producer of DAPPs, which uses Ethereum to create identity verification is the organization Oraclize. It has created a DAPP to solve your customer problem, which is at the heart of identity verification. This particular DAPP comes from Estonia, however, it can be expected that other countries will also adopt this. The organization Thomson Reuters is creating another dAPP for identity verification using Ethereum.

Creating wallets for crypto currency: A *wallet* for cryptocurrency is an electronic container, which is secure and stores, transmits, and allows the deposit of cryptocurrency. There are cryptocurrency exchanges that create wallets so you can deposit the cryptocurrency you purchased from them. It is an unfortunate fact that exchanges are a choice target for hackers, so it is not recommended to keep coins in these wallets. There are some cases where hackers successfully penetrated exchanges, and you are strongly advised to deposit your money elsewhere.

Ethereum lends itself to the creation of wallets; it is fair to say that a wallet is a smart contract. Some of the best-known wallets have been created using

Ethereum. Such wallets include Jaxx, which is a web wallet; KeepKey, which is a hardware wallet; Ledger Nano S, which is also a hardware wallet.

Smart contracts will create a peer-to-peer economy: It will be possible for two or more parties to conduct business directly without the use of an intermediary. This is no pipe dream; there are models of and actual applications to the insurance and other industries in existence.

Airbnb and Uber stand as two organizations which have used modern technology to disrupt accepted practice. Advocates of the peer-to-peer economy see smart contracts as a way of displacing Airbnb and Uber from their current role, essentially an intermediary, and allowing people to trade directly.

Crowdfunding new projects: Blockchain, such as Ethereum, will significantly increase the funding necessary for the development of new products and services. Currently, established companies such as Kickstarter offer methods allowing small investors to pool their funds for new projects.

These companies, being centralized and in complete control can charge high fees. Ethereum smart contracts, with its blockchain distributed network, can do away this model.

The entertainment industry is ripe for this as it would enable small scale investors in films and other media to get some reward, something that is currently very hard for them to obtain. It would make the financing and publicity for independent films much simpler than it currently is.

The Internet of Things (IoT): The Internet of Things (IoT) involves applying the connectivity provided by the Internet to the infrastructure of the home and also the country. Ethereum and its smart contracts are tailor-made for this.

Projects creating smart contracts for devices are predicted to proliferate. Gartner, the world's leading I.T. research company, has predicted that by 2020 there will be more than 20 billion connected devices. Such devices are being developed using Ethereum smart contracts. To name but three there is the Ethereum lightbulb, the Ethereum BlockCharge, which involves the charging of electric vehicles, and finally CryptoSeal, a tamper-resistant seal for ensuring the safety of drugs.

A great concern about widespread implementation of IOT is that in spite of the enormous potential benefits, hackers will have incredible opportunities to disrupt the lives of many people, in a way they have never been able to do before.

As well as being an integral part of the implementation of IoT, blockchain technologies, such as Ethereum, offer a way of dealing with hackers far more efficiently than in the past.

Archiving and file storage: The electronic archiving of documents has been thoroughly developed using centralized methods such as Google Drive, Dropbox, etc. These sites have always been at the mercy of hackers. Ethereum and its smart contracts offer a means of substantially reducing this threat and making the whole process of archiving better. There are many Ethereum projects which aim to do this.

Ethereum, with the use of its distributed network of nodes, can significantly improve the storage of data. It is important to note that there is no storage of the files on the blockchain. The storage occurs elsewhere, usually in the cloud. What smart contracts bring is storage that is a lot more secure than with any centralized system.

Protecting intellectual property: Blockchain enabled archiving will assist in greater protection of intellectual property than previously. At the moment, the protection of intellectual property such as music, books, and films has been very adversely affected by the advent of the Internet. Blockchain technology, such as that offered by Ethereum smart contracts, will significantly strengthen it. It will be far harder to steal copyrighted works with such contracts. Already there is an application called Ascribe, using such technology, which does this.

Crime: Lawbreakers have to camouflage the money gained from drugs, the sale of child pornography, extortion, etc. At present this can be done using offshore companies, gambling and fake bank accounts, among other methods. Ethereum smart contracts, when widely used, will make these ineffective and easily traced.

Social Media: At present, social media organizations such as Facebook, Instagram, Twitter, and others can freely harvest the personal data of their clients. This enables them to make billions of dollars. By the use of Ethereum smart contracts, social media users will be able to sell their personal data, if they wish. The famous university, MIT, is exploring such ideas.

The use of smart contracts in stock markets? Smart contracts in the trading of stocks and shares trading are potentially revolutionary in how they will affect current practices. The settlement could finish in seconds instead of the three days that is now needed. With smart contracts, peer-to-peer trading will become a reality, causing a complete revolution in the trading of stocks. Uses of smart contracts are being thoroughly explored in stock exchanges throughout the world including Australia, Japan, Germany, and the USA.

Using smart contracts in elections and polls: Smart contracts can vastly improve elections and polls. There is research currently underway, showing that elections could be run far cheaper and more reliably with a smart contract.

Checking the veracity of claims: Nowadays, people need assurance that the goods they buy are manufactured or harvested ethically. It is essential they are confident that the supplier did not involve slavery, exploitation, deforestation, the abuse of resources, etc. At present, corrupt suppliers can easily give false information to satisfy their customers. With the use of smart contracts, this kind of dishonesty will largely be a thing of the past. Already, there are situations where smart contracts are in use for this purpose, and there will be others.

Registration of land titles: Land registration titles are always problematic for those in real estate, such as owners of family homes, businesses, banks, developers, mortgage brokers, etc. The jobs of finding land titles then processing them is expensive in money and time. Ethereum, with its smart contracts, provides a solution for this task. Throughout the world, trials are being conducted to bring this to fruition.

Enabling Privacy and Anonymity: There are Ethereum projects to develop smart contracts, which allow anonymous communication between parties and preserve their privacy. Whether any such solution could be permanent is debatable, in light of the terrorism, which is currently sweeping the world.

Do you think the future of Ethereum is always going to be bright? Problems could arise in the future as a result of the split in the Ethereum world discussed earlier.

Advocates of either sort of Ethereum will always debate as to which version is best and why it is. At the moment there exist some minor differences of a technical nature that will become more significant with the passage of time, however a real disadvantage for Ethereum is that its coin Ether has NO hard cap. This means that ETH has no limit to its supply, although as we have already noted, there was a decision as Ethereum was beginning, that there would never be more than 18 million ETH produced annually. Ethereum Classic, however, has got a 230 million hard cap.

Is the existence or otherwise of a hard cap relevant? When something is allowed to grow, with no limits on growth, it often becomes worthless. Many are the times in history of governments expanding the supply of money leading to very negative results. When the number of the coin has a hard cap, then its value increases. Given the limited supply of Ethereum Classic (ETC), the chances of it ever becoming worthless are very few.

Despite this, the opportunities presented by the Ethereum project are very enticing for large organizations. Thirty of them, including the banks J.P. Morgan, Chase and Banco Santander and technology giants Microsoft and Intel have formed an organization called the Enterprise Ethereum Alliance. The purpose of this alliance is to build business-ready versions of software using Ethereum technology.

As one of the original attractions of blockchain was the exclusion of banks from the creation of money it is hard to see such organizations embracing something, one of whose avowed aims was their exclusion from money.

Chapter Six: Ethereum KeyPlayers and Technical Infrastructure

The Ethereum infrastructure has broad distribution. We have discussed the computers called nodes, among which are the miners, and their essential role in the Ethereum blockchain. There is also an Ethereum community dedicated to the success of this massive project.

A very important person still deeply involved in Ethereum, is Vitalik Buterin, whose white paper in 2014 started the Ethereum project. During the short life of Ethereum some key players have left, one such person was Gavin Wood lead developer in the C++ computer language. His replacement was Christian Reitweissner, creator of the Solidity computer language, expressly created for smart contracts. Other key personnel is Taylor Gerring who is the director of technology; Martin Becze who is the head of JavaScript client developments; Fabian Vogel Steller who is the head of dApp development; Alex Vander Sandy, who is the head missed developer and Viktor Tron, who is the leading Swarm developer. Swarm is heavily involved with artificial intelligence.

Despite these leading lights, the development of Ethereum code is a community effort. An Ethereum Foundation is leading the development of Ethereum. It is a not-for profit company headquartered in the city of Zug, Switzerland, mentioned before. The foundation has a governing board whose executive director is Ms. Ming Chan and whose members are Buterin himself, Jeffrey Wilcke and David Ben Key who, unlike Buterin and Wilcke, is not a professional programmer but rather a lawyer.

The rollout of Ethereum is not yet complete it is currently on Metropolis version 3, with Serenity version 4 planned for next year.

Chapter Seven: How Do I Go About Investing In Ethereum?

There are several ways of investing in Ethereum, you could get employment by learning the necessary skills in using Ethereum or some similar blockchain, you could try mining Ether, your investment could be by the purchase of some Ether then selling it, and finally, you could invest in ICOs.

Employment in Ethereum: For people who are both good at programming and good mathematics then there are some fantastic opportunities available to them. Visiting the Indeed Employment in late August 2017 revealed seven jobs where Ethereum skills were required and the salary was more than $150,000 annually, for slightly lower but still significant remuneration there were a lot more jobs.

If freelancing, rather than full-time work, appeals more to you then consider this at Upwork, a site for freelancers: the following position for more than thirty hours a week at an excellent rate.

Searching for a software architect for the design of a program that analyzes past financial data from the cryptocurrency markets. Coin data such as that from coinmarketcap.com and exchanges like poloniex and bittrex. The program should have analysis to allow the user to input variables and obtain ROI (return on investment) projections using algorithms the program will use to run against the data. The purpose of this is the discovery of trends in the cryptocurrency markets that will assist the decreasing of risks for investors and the obtaining of maximum returns.

Mining generally: The mining of cryptocurrencies started first with Bitcoin. When Bitcoin began during 2009, you could mine Bitcoins with an ordinary desktop computer. As time went by, the number of people using Bitcoin and the number mining for it massively increased and it was no longer possible to mine for Bitcoin in this way, even with several GPU (graphics processing units).

Anyone attempting to mine them on an ordinary computer, even one with a GPU, would cost more in electricity than the potential reward in coins.

If you intend to mine for Bitcoins at present time you need specialized equipment called ASIC's (Application Specific Integrated Circuits). Bitcoin mining hardware fits into a computer like a graphics card.

There are various brands of Bitcoin mining hardware. It is possible to spend a total of a few hundred dollars to many tens of thousands of dollars for such a machine.

What about mining Ether? This is very different to the situation applying with Bitcoin. Unlike Bitcoin, there is no specialized mining equipment for Ether. Ether is resistant to the sort of hardware used for mining Bitcoin. It is possible to mine Ether with a standard desktop computer but the task of doing so is much more efficient when we use a computer with a GPU. The GPU card should have at least 3 GB of RAM to mine Ether satisfactorily. Having purchased the necessary hardware then there is a need to download the program Geth, to connect the computer to the Ethereum network. If you use Geth, then you will have to use command line techniques to exploit it.

Once connected to the Ethereum network, it is necessary to install and use software for mining

Ether; a good program is Ethminer. You are far more likely to get a return on your investment if you join a mining pool than if you opt to mine alone. In such a pool miners combine their resources and are paid by their input.

Mining Ether should only be done after consideration of all the factors that are involved. If all you wish is to get some Ether, then you may well find that buying them from an exchange dealing in cryptocurrencies is simpler and has greater financial returns.

Trading with Ether on exchanges:

Cryptocurrency is receiving much publicity. This publicity has arisen because the value of Bitcoins has increased astronomically. However, Ether has done very well in 2017 as well. By late-August 2017, Ether reached a value in excess of $370 per coin from a value near $8 in Jan 2017; this is greater than a 4625% increase!! What does this mean? A sum of $100 invested in Ether in January 2016 when each ETH had a value of less than $1 would exceed $4625 in value now!

However, all is not necessarily safe; in late June 2017, there was an alarming situation where the value of 1 Ether fell to a value less than $0.10(US) on at least one large exchange! Fortunately for those who had substantial investments in Ether, the value rallied and had increased to over $350 in late August 2017.

Is Ether an investment to be made as soon as possible? A lot of experts think so, with many seeing nothing but an ever-increasing value against the dollar. Their argument runs that Ether and other cryptocurrencies appear peculiar now, however, recall how the major technology giants, such as Apple and Microsoft, began in the 1980s when it was thought by many that there would never be a use for personal computers. What a silly idea that proved to be; anyone who was far thinking enough then to invest substantially in them will have reaped rich rewards.

Before making any investment in Ethereum or any cryptocurrency, take the time and make an effort to learn everything you can about your planned investment. Always remember, if the value of an investment is rising now that does not mean it will always rise. Economic history has many examples of increases followed by steep falls; a very recent example was the U.S. real estate boom during the 2000s, up to 2007. Many are the times where values seem to go up forever as a direct result of outright dishonesty and massive exaggeration. When something goes up, it will usually come down.

Despite this warning, you may still be resolute in your desire to be involved in purchasing and trading in Ethereum. If that is the case, then you should start with the *exchanges* specializing in the business of cryptocurrencies. They should carefully help you start and should be willing to advise you as you venture forth.

Before beginning with one be sure to investigate it for its attitude and its reputation. If the personnel and exchange are unable or unwilling to respond to reasonable questions and are ignorant or arrogant, then use some other exchange. Professionalism is essential, an absence of it indicates an organization whose only concern is getting your money.

There are some excellent exchanges for beginners all over the world. Cex.io, Coinbase, and Kraken are all rated highly for people in the USA. Some countries are only just getting started in cryptocurrency and, usually, there is at least one local exchange who will help. No matter where you live you must carefully investigate them before making any investment. If you need information about exchanges, then do Google searches on *best cryptocurrency exchanges*.

Be warned that many exchanges will only trade with the major cryptocurrencies such as Bitcoin, Ether and Litecoin. Once you have chosen an exchange, you must fill in a whole lot of forms before they are allowed to accept you. In most countries, they are legally obliged to do this to make certain you are not a terrorist, criminal or other undesirable.

Ensure this book work is done this before you begin trading as if not done properly you could ruin a good trade.

With experience, you may acquire enough confidence to experiment with lesser known cryptocurrencies. Bittrex and Poloniex are exchanges that enable this. If you are in a less sophisticated country than the USA, you may have problems.

Do not rush, proceed slowly and with care until you know what you are doing. If you can find some trustworthy person to help as you start you will benefit. There are many Youtube tutorials on all aspects of cryptocurrency trading that you should watch as you proceed. No matter how you start, be very careful as it is so easy to make mistakes, and once you have lost your Ether or any other cryptocurrency it is lost forever!

Investing in ICOs: The acronym ICO represents *initial coin offering* and is like an IPO (initial public offering), with major differences in the regulations necessary for IPOs are not currently required in many countries for ICOs. This may soon cease to be the case as cryptocurrency becomes widely known and used.

Earlier we noted that the growth of blockchain is comparable to the explosion of Internet products and services during the late 1990s; some experts think it is going to be greater. Indeed, the market capitalization of all cryptocurrencies in 2016 saw increases of more than 50% and the growth in 2017 has been even larger.

Ethereum smart contracts are far more than just the transfer of digital currency. A lot of smart contract projects are said to improve significantly or entirely replace current processes. There are many conventional ways of doing things that are well past their use by date. These procedures and systems are due for replacement in the future, with smart contracts. The wise investor needs to identify those applications of Ethereum meeting a real need, and reject those that are unnecessary rubbish.

What makes a good smart contract? There are many smart contracts, which are full of bright features. **They seem to use Ethereum for no real purpose, to show how clever their developers are and to hoodwink investors**. Usually, these projects do not furnish a platform for further developments. What is meant by a platform? A platform is a smart contract that provides different services. A smart contract needs to be a lot more than electronic coin.

At the moment out of hundreds of existing and planned smart contracts, there are only 20 to 30 that meet a genuine need. The many that are left should not be considered for long-term investment. Bitcoin and Ethereum have set the standard for blockchain technologies for investment has been set by Bitcoin and Ethereum.

What are the uses of ICOs? With an ICO a company or organization attracts investors. The hope is they will purchase the 'currency' offered in the ICO, usually with ETH, often one of the other top cryptocurrencies such as BTC or even fiat currency.

ICOs are very plentiful at the moment with many of them on the website Coinschedule.

What happens at ICOs? Do a Google search on Coinschedule and then open that site. There is a table of Live Crowdfunds, and ICOs presented in different ways. You have a choice of cards, list and plates to view the ICOs on offer.

Open one and you will first see the company logo and beneath that a short description of the project. Then a list: Project type ...., Platform ....., link to the website, Category ....., Whitepaper ...., this latter title represents a significant feature. If an investor is contemplating an ICO, they should always read and try to understand the whitepaper. The whitepaper should give vital information about the project. Don't even consider investing in any ICO until you learn how to read a whitepaper.

Information provided should give a project overview so that you know what the outcome of the project will be, how advanced the project is, what the market for what's on offer is, what the tokens (coins) for sale are used for and how token holders can make money. There should be information about bonuses or bounties.

An important question is whether there is any mention of a hard cap or a soft cap. The maximum number of coins available is the hard cap. The number of coins that need to be sold for the ICO to be a success is the soft cap. The whitepaper should state how funds invested will be returned if the sale is a failure.

Readers of the whitepaper should be informed about the development team. If you are thinking about a large investment check those people listed very carefully. Check forums, social media, Google, etc. and be very thorough.

A whitepaper should analyze the competition. However, it is important to do your analysis though as sometimes what the whitepaper says does not reveal all that is pertinent. See how much competition there is actually and how well-placed the project is to meet the existing competition. Does what is on offer provide anything new?

As an example, let us have a look at Smart RE, an ICO, which when we looked at it was soon to finish.

Project type Token, Platform Ethereum and Wave,..

SmartRE aims to provide a real estate platform that is decentralized and tokenized. It will give US homeowners an opportunity to liquidate some of their home's equity without the creation of debt. Investors from all over the world will be able to buy into American real estate, without vast expenditure. The whole project is insured.

Let's look at another called Lampix; the platform is Ethereum,

The short description indicates artificial intelligence is the purpose of the project.

The whitepaper for Lampix is 85-page long. Unfortunately, it is not very well edited. This is a bad sign; it shows that despite their efforts the organizers did not even get an editor to process basic grammar.

As is so often the case, what is on offer could only be judged by someone with extensive knowledge of what is on offer. In this case, it was AI (artificial intelligence). The whitepaper describes problems in providing datasets of images for artificial intelligence in the field of augmented reality (AR). Solutions to this problem lie in a PIX ecosystem based on the Ethereum.

The Pix coins are used by those in AR, who use the Lampix system. Pix is the first Ethereum project for AR. The target for the ICO was $60 million, and raised before the ICO pre-sales had raised $200,000. The company saw a finish to the project by the end of 2018.

Pix leap frogs off an existing product Lampix, which can change any surface into a smart surface. There is a lot of space in the whitepaper given to the team developing this project.

The Pix project provides a platform for development, and there are depictions for future growth prospects. This white paper is very good at analyzing the competition to help potential investors reach a decision.

Considerable attention is devoted to the proposed use of the funds raised from the ICO. There is a clear blueprint of past and future steps.

After a quick read of this whitepaper, it was obviously very well detailed. However, I received advice that Pix was only relevant to AR. The advice given was not to invest in the Lampix ICO.

Some other ICOs have whitepapers that offer services, which are copies of services already in existence. Avoid these when investing.

Coinschedule only deals with reputable ICOs so to find a dodgy one I had to look elsewhere. It was not necessary to look far as a Google search for *ICO scam* revealed

An ICO for adult entertainment supposed to start July 10, 2017. Accepts ETH and BTC.

- *Has a Website: xxxxxxx*
- *Twitter: yyyyyyyy*

Supposed Founders:

- *ppppppp, <u>LinkedIn</u>**
- *mmmmmmm, <u>Github</u>*

*update: LinkedIn account not available

Consider the following facts: The whitepaper was a blatant copy of another and was 100% a copy

*update: later there was no link to the whitepaper which had been deleted from the website

The project leaders were so slack that they left links to the site they had copied.

The conclusion was that apart from spending a few hours making a beautiful looking website the whole scheme was a rip off!

Most people like quick returns and ICOs offer that. Currently, in the USA, organizers of ICOs are not regulated like venture capitalists. As a result, there is a need for caution. In an unregulated situation confidence men soon make an appearance, with all manner of get-rich proposals and unfortunately ICOs are currently very susceptible to these.

The SEC (Securities and Exchange Commission) has given warnings to potential investors in ICOs to be very wary of guaranteed investment schemes. Look carefully at promises of unusually high returns, unsought offers, any system that seems to be too good to be true (you can be sure it isn't), and any pressure to purchase without delay and sales people who are unlicensed.

What Proportion of Your Investment Portfolio Should Be Cryptocurrency Mining, Trading or ICOs?

Many factors will bear on this. The stories of people who made fortunes with only small investments in Bitcoin, Ethereum and other cryptocurrency are true. However, you must never forget that cryptocurrency is very volatile, and for huge returns, you must manage your investments actively.

Successful investment in these new products takes a lot of work. You cannot just purchase Ethereum and expect it to keep doubling in dollar value forever. Irrespective of what you do, <u>You Must Never Invest More Than You Can Afford To Lose</u>. This applies especially to those new to investing. Start with a small amount, like $100, until you know what you are doing; if you rush you can expect some financial unhappiness.

The younger you are, the safer it is to invest substantially in cryptocurrency. If you are under 30 years old then do not exceed 35% cryptocurrency, and have a minimum of 50% invested safely (be certain to be well advised as to what is safe). For those 30 – 40 years old then don't invest more than 20% in cryptocurrency and have least 60% invested safely. If you are over 40 years old, then you need to think seriously about retirement, and hence no more than 10% cryptocurrency, with a minimum 70% invested safely.

These suggestions include ICOs but unless you know an industry inside out and can see how smart contracts could benefit it then leave ICOs alone.

Conclusion

This brings to an end this introductory book about Ethereum.

We have tried to show how Ethereum has the potential to be far more than Bitcoin. The book has shown much that can be done with this amazing technology. There has been an in-depth discussion about it.

You have been given reasons to make the decision for investment in it but to be very careful if you do so and proceed slowly.

Good luck!

Other Books

- **HOW TO GET FILTHY RICH:** UNLEASH THE BEAST IN YOU AND BECOME A POWER PLAYER

Here's a Preview of the book:

Introduction

I want to thank you and congratulate you for downloading the book, "**HOW TO GET FILTHY RICH**". We want to become rich and its not even by choice, we are driven by necessity. To eat lavishly, to go to a nice restaurant, to wear better clothes, we need money. To endure torturous heat in summer, we need an air conditioner, we are paying so much money for cool air to have it switched on for hours, we need to bear these fat electricity bills. Money is in bare necessities. It's in the minimum of human joy to the maximum of human comforts. Actually, the very definition of the human comfort now is measured in the terms of money. A mere vacation gets reduced by the limitations of your pockets, luxury is not synonymous with royalty, it's synonymous with better and comfortable.

Let me clear off some of the myths first, there is no formula for those lazy people who just want to sit in their living rooms, stay in their bed, dreaming if they can get a formula, not bigger than an inch, which they can then apply and change their lives and become millionaires; Well I have bad news it's never going to happen. If such a thing existed, we would all be millionaires. Here's news for you: There are no get rich quick schemes, those are lies, bullshit, nonsense, created to take some of your money instead. These are scams, Second, there are no ways you can become a millionaire in a year. If you sitting in your house clueless about your future, not a single book or course can make you a millionaire in a year. Those who become one are actually working on their ideas for many years prior to their success.

Now coming to the point, you want to earn money like a champion. I will give you seven chapters. Follow them, follow them patiently and passionately and the income your bank account might see a substantial growth within a year.

This is my guarantee because I am not asking anything in return, all I want is you to achieve the best you deserve.

Thanks again for downloading this book, **I hope you enjoy it!**

Chapter 1

Smart Work Vs Hard Work (Labor)

Smart work doesn't mean skipping work and lazing around. Labor does not mean strict hard work. Most people have dangerous potentials, but their energy, dedication and focus are being wasted by working towards the wrong direction.

For example, you have the potential to give your 100% and that's what you usually give at your workplace, but you are only rewarded for the 10%, doesn't matter if you give 20, 30, 40%, it's all going unrewarded, why are you then still doing this?

Two big reasons are the **APPROVAL** and hope of **PROMOTION**. We are either looking up to somebody and in that amazement which fazes the logic and reasoning in you, because that's what following does to the mind, you are blindly sticking to that company. You are thinking, my boss loves me, why should I ever leave that place, despite the fact that if you ever tried applying elsewhere, you can easily get a better deal. But we have discovered a home like environment, and that is the greatest trick the smartest bosses pull. They know that you are looking for approval, and to them you are the cash creating machine. Why would they let you go? In other case, we are too hopeful, we are impressing these people in hopes that one day they will recognize my hard work. So, In our heads we believe that one day they might give me a promotion on the basis of my hard work. That's a belief my friend. You are not in school anymore waiting for your teacher to recognize your potential. These people don't give a fuck about you. They have already seen many just like you come and go; you are just another replacement. If there aren't any incentives for your extra work beyond the required 10%, save your 90% for yourself.

Be SMART, don't be a FOLLOWER. In corporate world, nobody gives a fuck about YOU! Don't build FALSE hopes in your head and present yourself to disappointment.

You work only for yourself. And that is what smart work is, when you work for yourself, labor is when you definitively get paid 100 bucks for lifting bricks the entire day, no matter what.

Another input I would love to add is, We humans are gifted with a thing called intuition, and we spend majority of our lives ignoring it. Intuition isn't born out of insecurities, it's the spider sense in your mind, it's a trigger your brain pulls every time it sees a need to protect you or warn you. But most of us push it so far down that we can barely even hear it, because we choose to govern our actions on the basis of feelings.

For example, in relationships, We say: I have put my trust in her and she promised that she will never break my heart, so I am going to believe what she says, even though your brain is telling you. Sending you warning signs, that something is not making sense; You are being screwed; What we do is, we wait until we do get screwed completely. In professional life, your intuitions will constantly tell you the logical conclusion of your observations, deep inside you will know that your capabilities are not being recognized or valued in this place. Which is why, you need to stop attaching yourself emotionally with people, so you can leave the place without the emotional ordeal.

Does smart work mean skipping work? Not at all. Those who skip work and feel pride for doing so, stop at 10. I am asking you to do your 100%, including the percentage required at work.
For example, if you are earning $500, extend your work that satisfies that amount. Where do you apply rest of your efficiency? On yourself. We always know what our weaknesses are, why not focus on them? Try to improve yourself. It will help you immensely.
Most people fear job interviews because they fail to present themselves brilliantly.
Your impression on important people who have the power to change your lives should be impeccable.
There are many people who successfully pull off doing 10% at their job, but then, they choose laziness. They are celebrating skipping

work so much that they ultimately develop shitty work habits.

And lastly, be opportunistic. Paint targets in your mind. You must always know the right person to impress, and when you get the opportunity, blow their minds away, but for that you need to have your weapons ready.

I will be honest with you, most people around you don't have a clue what they are doing; Others are satisfied with what they have and then there are those who are happy being followers.

These are not the dreamers, they are the workforce. You work for yourself. If you are not getting rewarded, screw that job in your mind, do the minimum, so you can get your increment by the end of the year, and get the shit out of there.

That was chapter 1. And before moving on to the next chapter, I want you to do something. As an exercise, I want you to start building this mindset, the mindset that now you have to, at any cost, become unconquerable, which is why I have broken this book into different chapters. Consume it at your own pace.

Chapter 2

GIVE YOUR 100%

Why do I focus so much on 100%?
Because this is the real game. You want to stay mediocre, ordinary, never truly achieve what you want, stay the same; But as I have already said in the previous chapter, your surrounding is not putting their 100% either, so that gives you a natural advantage over them. Take that as a blessing. Now what does 100% really mean? To most it might sound like extreme labor. You have a natural potential, call it energy, daily capacity, efficiency. What I mean by that is, you are with or without choice, fulfilling or using the 100% of that potential

every single day. The one you call winner, consciously plans and chooses the activities in which he will be participating and using that potential. The one call loser, does not give a shit. You have met those people, "I don't give a shit." "I don't even have things planned for the next hour, how silly of you to ask me what would I be doing tomorrow?"

You have heard this. Maybe in a different language, but you have heard this line being said with pride. This line if not said as a joke, makes the person a moron. You don't believe me? Ask any person who is working with the motivation to become a millionaire, he will have his shit planned in a tight schedule. You want to be a rich man? Figure out in a paper where you use all your energy on daily basis. If you need any help, let me provide you that as well, here are some of my guesses: Girls, Texting, Porn, Films, Gaming, Tv shows, More texting, Gaming apps, Internet browsing, Youtube, Facebook, Instagram, Snapchat, Get togethers, Clubbing, Partying, Malls, Planned dinners, Hang-outs, Drinking, Smoking, Drugs. This list might sound very cliched and stupid, because you actually know that these things are a time waste, but despite that fact in this list, you will find where your remaining 90% efficiency goes. Then you can argue how can all these things drain my energy? They hardly require any physical work. Well, something more important than physical energy required to become better is called mental energy. When you aimlessly feed your mind information that is serving you no purpose other than entertainment, gossip and time pass, do not fool yourself into believing that your mind is shut off.

Your mind is not a sentient being, it will process and consume whatever you feed it, that is its function. Which is why ultimately it will get too tired for studies, work, learning, brainstorming, creative thinking, or any productive engagements.

For example, when you watch a movie at a theater, don't you talk or think about it for the entire day? Why do you think that happens, after all that movie was entertainment. It happens because you have fed your mind 2-3 hours of information with the greatest focus known to man. When you watch a movie, you shut off all the other issues where your mind generally engages, which is why your mind processes the movie and generates thoughts about it the entire day.

Take another example, gaming. What happens when you game consistently for 6-7 hours a day? You get dreams of playing the same game in your sleep. Why? The same applies. The focus is constant if not more. But instead of 2-3 hours, it's 8 or 10. It's such an overload for your brain, that it completely takes over your unconscious.

I can go on and on about every single activity in that list. How is it not affecting your mental energy?

Now, you might ask, are you asking me to not watch any movie or my favorite TV shows?

NO. Prioritize. Introduce this word in your life. Let me tell you one thing, the objective of movies, TV shows, facebook, all these apps and shit, is not to provide you with entertainment; it's to make tonnes of money off you. They are fulfilling their objective and their motive is selfish. Why are you helping them endlessly when it is not the other way round?

When you figure out on which things you are wasting your potential, Make a change, and this is the first change I am asking you to make in this book. The ratio of 10% work and 90% helping millionaires make money, girls, and other shit, should change to 90% work and 10% fun.

Work for yourself and on yourself. Most people want to better themselves, but they get satisfied at getting the answer, because they find that the solution is asking them to work, there are exercises, you would have to make efforts. And most of us just want magical solutions, little formulas, an exercise that takes seconds to fix your problem.

Why is 100% important?

The world is actually a simple place, there are opportunities that will significantly increase the state of your bank account, to get those opportunities you need to be prepared, preparation does not happen overnight- which you are used to doing; and therefore, you remain part of the stupid workforce.

Another problem is, most people stop doing their 90% bullshit, but still waste their time in the vacuum they have created, as the percentage of the work still remains 10%.

You can get rid of the apps, girls, addictions, but it is still useless if you don't know what to do. No need to worry, I have got it covered for you in the next chapters. But I am pretty sure you do know what are the things you need to do to grow, succeed, and tear the competition apart. So be patient. The first thing I am asking you to do is, management. Manage your addictions. Don't get rid of them yet, learn how to control them first.
Acknowledgment of your problems in itself is the first stage to recovery. You are close to victory.

Take some time out today, and find out , acknowledge, and accept all the things you do on a daily basis that take away a lot of your time, and give you nothing in return. Just do that. This is a re-evolution. You are going to become a conqueror after this book is over.

Go to Amazon Author Page of "BRIAN T. SMITH" to read the full book.